Dedication

We dedicate this book to all the amazing moms and mother figures!

We see you.

Acknowledgments

We are thankful for our Moms, grandmothers, mother figures, and female role models in our lives. Special shoutout to our dear friends:

- Andrea Bastiani Archibald, Ph.D. (Developmental Psychologist, former Executive of Girl Scouts of the USA and Raising Awesome Girls, and mom)

- Dr. Rachel Dew (Doctor of Integrative Wellness and Self-Development Author, and mom)

- Colleen Marchi (Psychologist, Children's book author, Military spouse, and mom)

- Laura Boram (Waldorf teacher extraordinaire, and mom)

You mamas uplifted us along the entire book writing journey and gave us the confidence to keep going!

I never saw my Mom's cape, but...

I see her wash and brush her hair.
She makes doing things that are hard for me to do look so easy.

I see her make her bed in the morning.
She makes staying organized look so easy.

I see her work in the garden.
She makes growing food look so easy.

I see her wash all the dishes in the sink.
She makes cleaning look so easy.

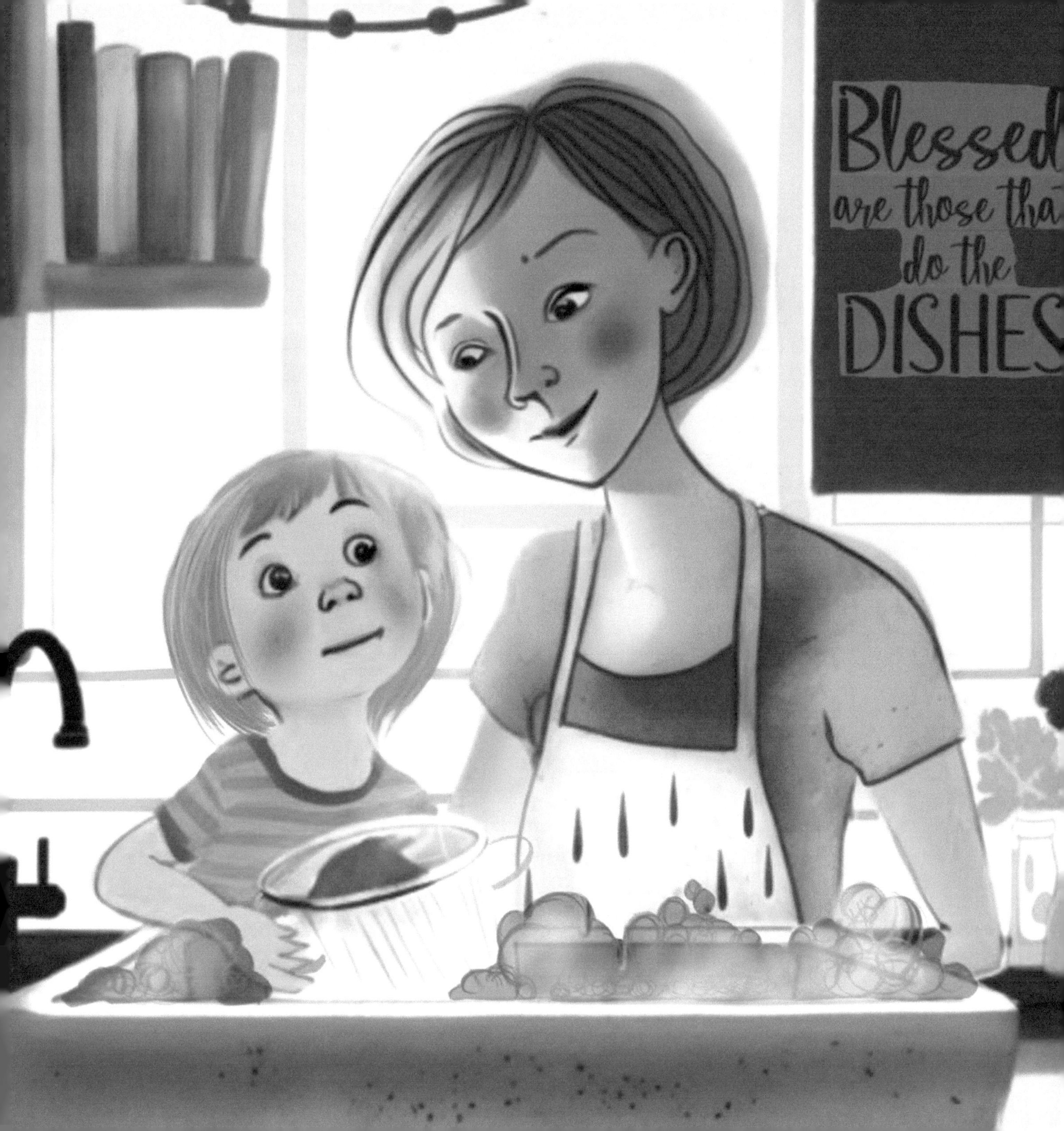
Blessed
are those tha
do the
DISHES

I see her meditate and do yoga.
She makes stretching and just being look so easy.

I see her take her vitamins every day.
She makes taking care of herself look so easy.

I see her enjoy fresh foods whenever she can.
She makes eating healthy look so easy.

I see her whisper a 'thank you' to her water.
She makes being grateful look so easy.

I see her go on walks every night - rain or shine.
She makes keeping good habits look so easy.

I see her knit for the first time.
She makes learning something new look so easy.

I see her take the bus to work when we didn't have a car.
She makes saving money look so easy.

I see her share things we weren't using anymore.
She makes giving look so easy.

I see her on a Zoom call with a lot of people.
She makes being a boss look so easy.

I see her prepare meals for us after long workdays.
She makes cooking at home look so easy.

I see her make soup for Grandpa.
She makes taking care of others look so easy.

I see her sad sometimes.
She makes going through tough times look so easy.

I see her wrap me in her scarf to make me warmer.
She makes knowing when to put me first look so easy.

I see her dance at a wedding.
She makes being confident look so easy.

I see her struggle to ride a bike,
but she biked around with me anyway.
She makes sticking through it look so easy.

I see her work hard on her big presentation.
She makes preparing look so easy.

I see her study on weekends and nights.
She makes growing look so easy.

I see her make birthdays and milestones feel so special.
She makes celebrating others look so easy.

I never saw your cape, but...
Mommy, I see you make everything look so easy.

If you could only see yourself through my eyes,
through the eyes of a little one in this big world
that is made for big people!

None of those things that you do are easy for me.
I remember when you told me once that they were not
easy for you either in the beginning.

Some things are still not easy for you to juggle
and do as perfectly as I know you want them to be.

But Mommy, you do them anyway.

I never saw your cape, but ... I see you.
You are there every day making it happen.

I never saw your cape, but...

I see you _____

You make _____ look so easy.

I see you _____

You make_____ look so easy.

I see you _____

You make_____ look so easy.

I see you _____

You make _____ look so easy.

You make everything look so easy. I see you.

Happy Your-day!

Love, _____

Photo area:
Mom and child or just Mom doing something she loves

About the Author

I never saw my mom's cape, but ... is co-authored by Skye + Fam: Skye, Payel, and Joe Farasat.

Skye Farasat, age nine, co-authored her second book I never saw my mom's cape, but ... with her family. Skye came up with the initial concept of the book while secretly observing her Mom brushing tangles and knots out of her hair. In this book, she serves as a little guide who reminds us of the many little (and big) things that Moms (and mother figures) do for their families. We may think that the little things go unnoticed and the big things are just little; however, Skye reminds us that our children are always observing us and soaking it all in. Skye has been meditating with her parents since she was a baby. She shares her simple yet powerful technique of using observation as one way to remain mindful and thankful for your mom. Skye is a fourth grader and has been a student of Waldorf education since age four. Since Waldorf's pedagogy centers around inner work, Skye leaves a special space at the end of the book for kids to be inspired to write about how they see their moms.

Payel and Joe Farasat are Skye's mommy and daddy, and they helped edit the book. They are Financial Services executives, certified in coaching, consulting, and mindfulness.

About the Book

A book about celebrating Moms every day! I Never Saw My Mom's Cape, But ... reminds us of the many little (and big) things that Moms (and mother figures) do for their families. We may think that the little things go unnoticed and the big things are just little; however, this book reminds us that our children are always observing us and soaking it all in.

The book leaves a special space at the end for kids to be inspired to write about how they see and appreciate their mom. A heartfelt and thoughtful personal dedication makes for a memorable gift for Mom, especially on Mother's Day, birthday, or really any day!

Made in United States
Troutdale, OR
03/30/2024

18807099R00036